WAVES

Physical Science for Kids

ANDI DIEHN

Illustrated by Shululu

Nomad Press
A division of Nomad Communications
10 9 8 7 6 5 4 3 2 1

This book was manufactured by CGB Printers,
North Mankato, Minnesota, United States
March 2018, Job #240596

ISBN Softcover: 978-1-61930-635-6
ISBN Hardcover: 978-1-61930-633-2

Educational Consultant, Marla Conn

Questions regarding the ordering of this book should be addressed to
Nomad Press
2456 Christian St.
White River Junction, VT 05001
www.nomadpress.net

Printed in the United States.

Other titles in this series:

Check out more titles at www.nomadpress.net

Waves in water, waves in wheat.

Waves at a game: "Stand up! Take a seat!"

Waves in your hair, waves with your hand,

Powerful waves under the land.

Make waves in a string,
then stretch it taut,

Waves are everywhere, whether
we see them or not!

A wave is a way of saying
"HELLO!"

Where else can you
find waves?

Swimming in the ocean
is fun and salty!

What happens when a
wave comes? You might
find yourself upside down
and downside up.

You can find waves in oceans, lakes, ponds, and even puddles.

Watch out for the big ones!

If you float on your back in a pond, do the waves move you to shore? After a long time they might. But water in a wave isn't moving across the pond. Water in a wave is moving up and down, up and down.

TRY THIS!

Fill a sink or a bucket with water. Float a ball or piece of foam on the water. With your fingers, make some waves in the water!

» What happens to the ball?   » Does it move up and down?
» Does it travel?   » Does it go anywhere?

4

Waves happen because of energy.

Energy is an invisible force that travels
as a wave. When you see waves in
water, it's the energy that's moving
toward the shore, not the water.

Have you ever watched
a cat play with a
dangling string?

What happens when
the cat catches the string,
pulls, and lets it go?

WAVES!

Have you ever been to a baseball game? The people watching the game make a giant wave with their bodies.

TRY THIS!

Stretch a Slinky across a room. Shake one end of the Slinky.

» What do you see?
» Where is the energy coming from to make the wave?

Around and around goes the human wave!

The people aren't moving anywhere except up and down. Their up-and-down motion creates a wave.

9

When the wind blows, waves move across a field of wheat. Does the wheat move its roots?

No! Every stalk of wheat stands in place.

Just the top part moves, back and forth, back and forth.

Flags from different countries wave in the breeze.

Can you find
the flag for
your country?

Have you ever jumped on a trampoline?

If you could draw the motion of your jumps,
what would that look like on paper?

You'd find waves on your paper!

You might not be able to see the waves in the air as you jump, but the motion you are making is drawing waves as you move.

There are lots of invisible waves
in the air. You can't see them,
but they're all around you.

A wave is how light moves through the air.

Light travels in waves from the sun to planet Earth. We can't see the waves, but we can see the light! This is light energy traveling in the form of a wave.

Do you ever
cook food in a
microwave?

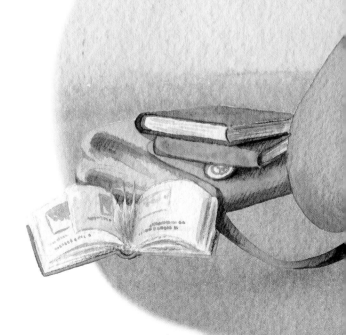

Do you ever
talk to someone
on a cell phone?

Do you
ever listen
to a radio?

Microwaves, cell phones, and radios
all use waves. These are more
invisible waves made of energy.

"Hello," says Mom on the phone.
"Remember to do your homework!"

**You can hear her
because of waves.**

Sound moves in waves, too. When a dog barks, the sound of the bark spreads through the air in waves. When the waves reach your ears, you can hear the sounds.

What other sounds do you hear?

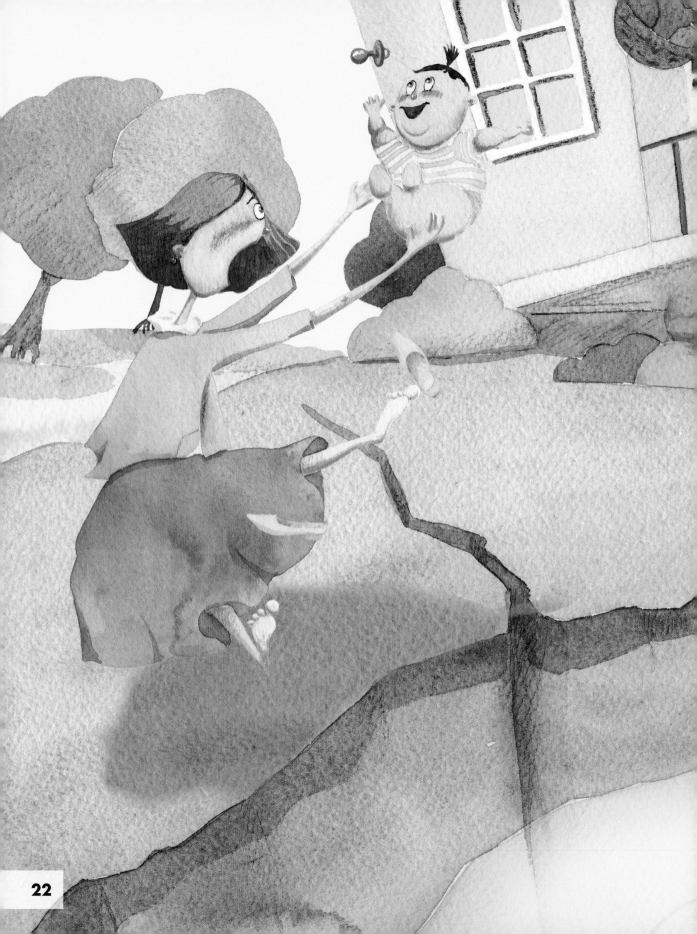

Have you ever felt an earthquake?
The earth feels like a wave is
passing through it. And that's
exactly what is happening!
Invisible waves move through the
ground and make it rumbly.

This is energy moving through the earth.

Just like waves going through water,
waves going through dirt don't
make the dirt move very far.
The land goes up and down,
up and down, up and down.
But the earth doesn't move
to a different address!

A wave is a way of
saying "Goodbye!"

"GOODBYE!"

GLOSSARY

address: where you live.

cell phone: a telephone you can carry around with you.

energy: the power to work, grow, move, and do things.

invisible: unable to be seen.

light: something that makes it so we can see.

microwave: an oven that cooks food with waves.

radio: a device that uses waves to make sound.

wave: a curving movement in water, air, ground, or other object.